STRUM IT GUITAR

AUTHENTIC CHORDS
ORIGINAL KEYS
COMPLETE SONGS

THE Beatles Favorites

Contents

Cover Photo © Apple Corps Ltd
Used by Permission

ISBN 0-634-01886-8

HAL•LEONARD®
CORPORATION
7777 W. BLUEMOUND RD. P.O. BOX 13819 MILWAUKEE, WI 53213

Visit Hal Leonard Online at
www.halleonard.com

HOW TO USE THIS BOOK

Strum It!™ is the series designed especially to get you playing (and singing!) along with your favorite songs. The idea is simple—the songs are arranged using their original keys in *lead sheet* format, giving you the chords for each song, beginning to end. The melody and lyrics are also shown to help you keep your spot and sing along.

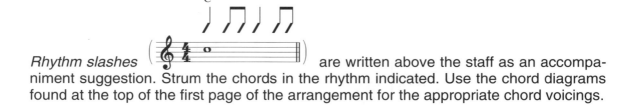

Rhythm slashes are written above the staff as an accompaniment suggestion. Strum the chords in the rhythm indicated. Use the chord diagrams found at the top of the first page of the arrangement for the appropriate chord voicings.

Additional Musical Definitions

⊓	• Downstroke
∨	• Upstroke
D.S. al Coda	• Go back to the sign (𝄋), then play until the measure marked *"To Coda,"* then skip to the section labelled *"Coda."*
D.C. al Fine	• Go back to the beginning of the song and play until the measure marked *"Fine"* (end).
cont. rhy. sim.	• Continue using similar rhythm pattern.
N.C.	• Instrument is silent (drops out).
𝄆 𝄇	• Repeat measures between signs.
1. 2.	• When a repeated section has different endings, play the first ending only the first time and the second ending only the second time.

Can't Buy Me Love

Words and Music by John Lennon and Paul McCartney

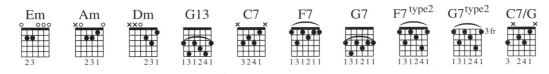

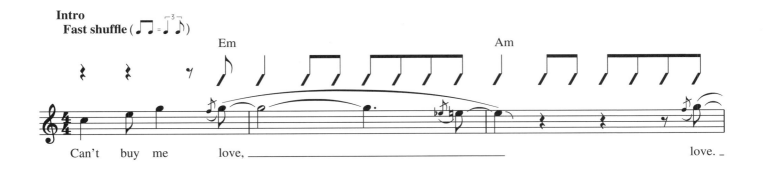

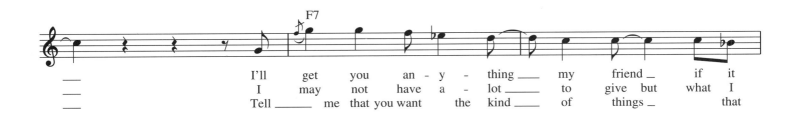

makes   you   feel   al - right. ____   'Cause   I   don't   care   too
got   I'll   give   to   you. ____
mon - ey   just   can't   buy. ____

To Coda ⊕ |1.

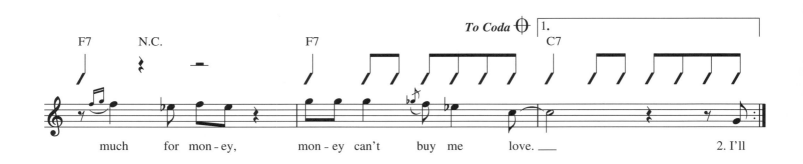

much   for   mon - ey,   mon - ey   can't   buy   me   love. ____   2. I'll

|2.

Bridge

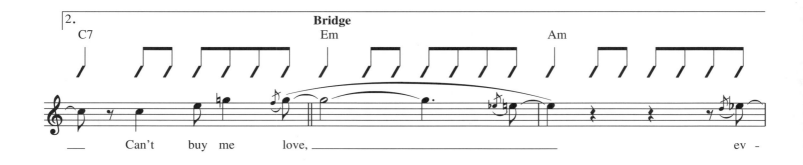

____   Can't   buy   me   love, _____   ev -

cont. rhy. sim.

- 'ry - bod - y   tells   me   so.   Can't   buy   me   love, _____   uh,

|3.

no,   no,   no, ____   no. _____   3. Say ____   Ow! _____

Guitar Solo

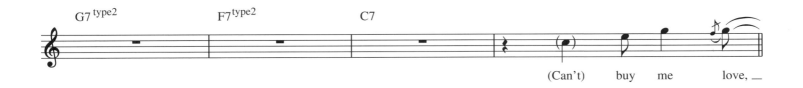

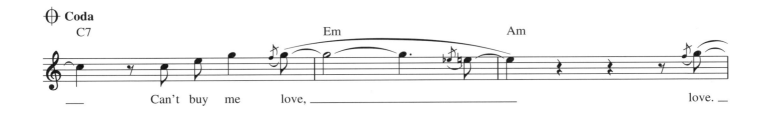

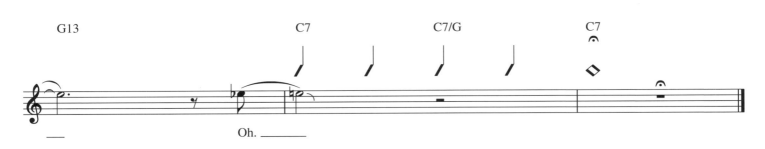

The Continuing Story of Bungalow Bill

Words and Music by John Lennon and Paul McCartney

Hey   Bun-ga-low Bill, __   what did you kill, __   Bun-ga-low Bill? __

Hey   Bun-ga-low Bill, __   what did you kill, __   Bun-ga-low Bill? __   1. He

1. went out ti-ger hunt-ing with his el-e-phant __ and gun. ____
2. Deep in the jun-gle where the might-y ti-ger lies, ____
3. The child-ren asked hi mif to kill __ was not a sin. ____

In case of ac-ci-dents __ he al-ways took his mom. ____   He's the
Bill and his el-e-phants were tak-en by sur-priese. ____
"Now when he looked sofierce," his mom-my but-ted itn, ____

all A-mer-i-can, bul-let head-ed, Sax-on mo-ther's son.
So Cap-tain Mar-vel zapped him right be-tween the eyes. ___
"If looks could kill it would-'ve been us in-stead of him."

1. All the child-ren sing. _

2. All the child-ren sing. _

3. All the child-ren sing.

Chorus

*Hey Bun-ga-low Bill, ___ what did you kill, ___ Bun-ga-low Bill? ____

*whistling 4th time

Hey Bun-ga-low Bill, ___ what did you kill, ___ Bun-ga-low Bill? ____

4.

Free time

Eh up!

Eight Days a Week

Words and Music by John Lennon and Paul McCartney

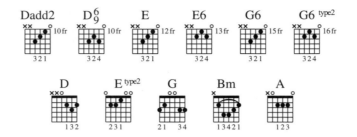

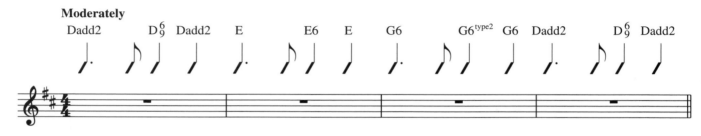

Intro

Moderately

1., 3. Oo, I need your love, babe, _ guess you know it's true. _
2., 4. *See additional lyrics*

Hope you need my love, babe, _ just like I need you. __

Chorus

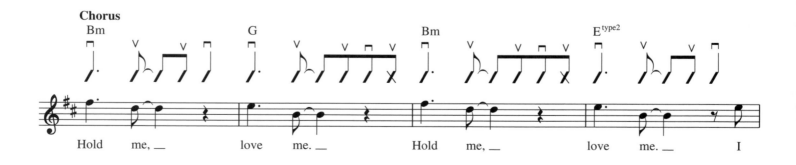

Hold me, _ love me. _ Hold me, _ love me. _ I

Additional Lyrics

2., 4. Love you ev'ryday, girl,
Always on my mind.
One thing I can say, girl,
Love you all the time.

From Me to You

Words and Music by John Lennon and Paul McCartney

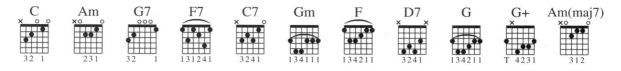

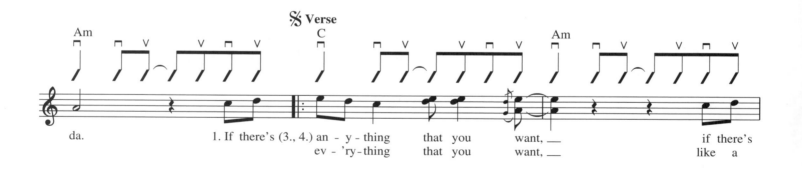

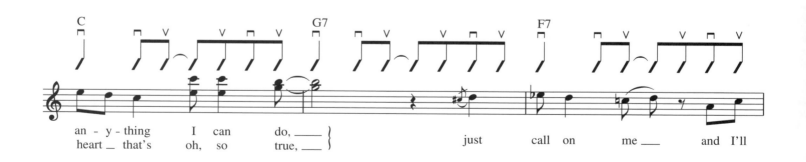

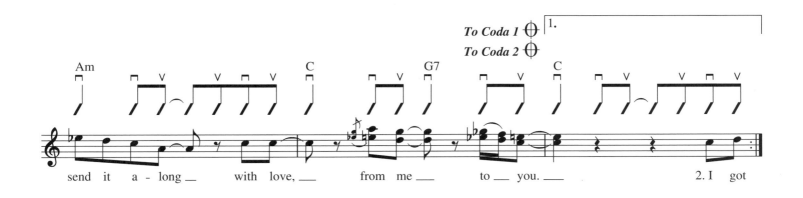

To Coda 1
To Coda 2
1.

send it a - long ___ with love, ___ from me ___ to ___ you. ___ 2. I got

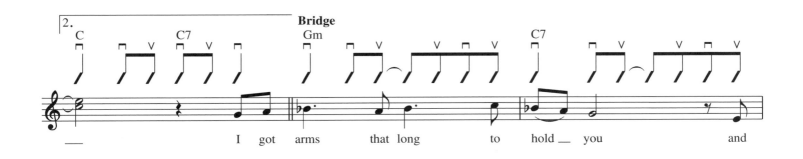

2. **Bridge**

___ I got arms that long to hold ___ you and

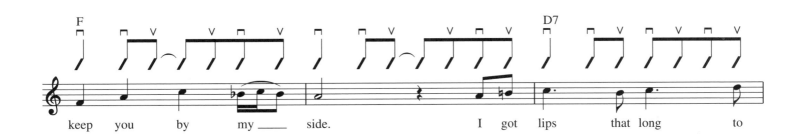

keep you by my ___ side. I got lips that long to

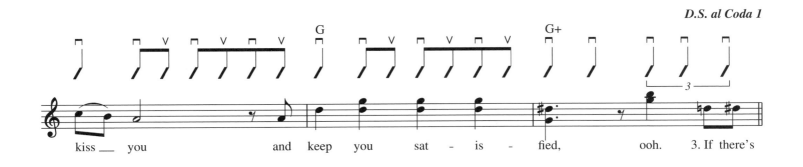

D.S. al Coda 1

kiss ___ you and keep you sat - is - fied, ooh. 3. If there's

Coda 1

Harmonica/Guitar Solo

___ From ___ me ___

11

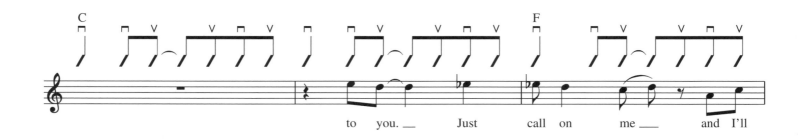

to you. ___ Just call on me ___ and I'll

send it a - long ___ with love, ___ from me ___ to you. ___ I got

Bridge

arms that long to hold ___ you and keep you by my ___ side. I got

lips that long to kiss ___ you and keep you sat - is - fied, ooh. 4. If there's

Coda 2

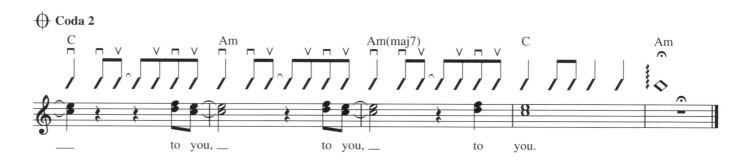

___ to you, ___ to you, ___ to you.

A Hard Day's Night

Words and Music by John Lennon and Paul McCartney

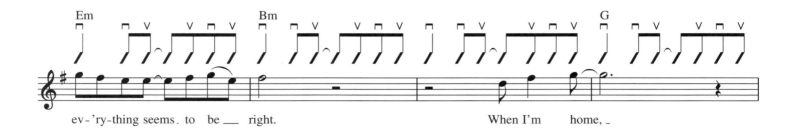

ev-'ry-thing seems. to be ___ right.   When I'm   home, ___

To Coda 2 ⊕   *D.S. al Coda 1*

feel - ing you hold - ing me tight, ___   tight, ___   yeah. ___ 3. It's been a

⊕ **Coda 1**

___   Ow! ___

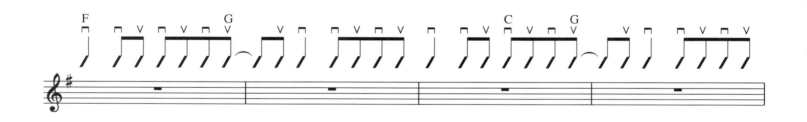

4. So why on earth should I moan ___ 'cause when I

D.S.S. al Coda 2

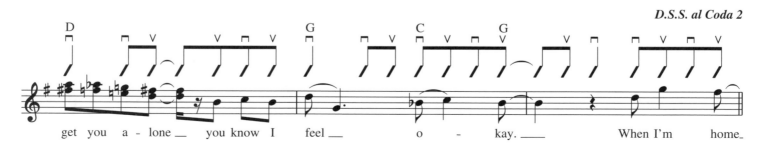

get you a - lone ___ you know I feel ___   o - kay. ___   When I'm home_

feel al - right. ____

Hey Jude

Words and Music by John Lennon and Paul McCartney

Capo I

Verse
Rock Ballad

*Symbols in parentheses represent chord names respective to capoed guitar
and do not reflect actual sounding chords.

1. Hey Jude, don't make it bad, take a sad song and make it bet-ter. Re-
   Jude, don't be a-fraid, you were made to go out and get her. The

mem-ber to let her in-to your heart, then you can start
min-ute you let her un-der your skin, then you be-gin

to make it bet ter. 2. Hey
to make it bet -

ter.

And an-y-time you feel the pain,

*Symbols in parentheses represent chord names respective to capoed guitar.
Symbols above reflect actual sounding chords.

I Should Have Known Better

Words and Music by John Lennon and Paul McCartney

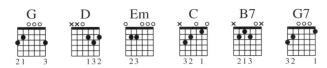

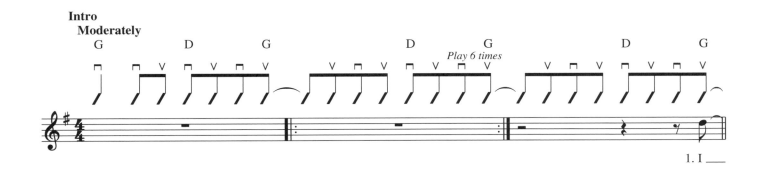

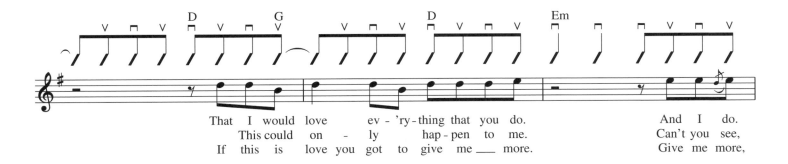

19

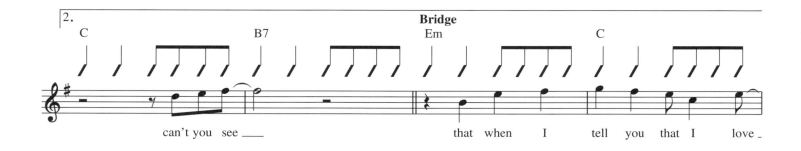

can't you see ___   that when I tell you that I love ___

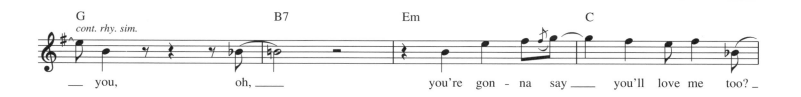

___ you,   oh, ___   you're gon - na say ___ you'll love me too? ___

Oh. ___   And when I ask you to be mi -

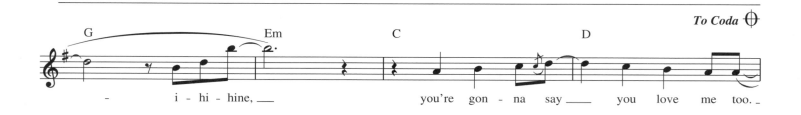

- i - hi - hine, ___   you're gon - na say ___ you love me too. ___

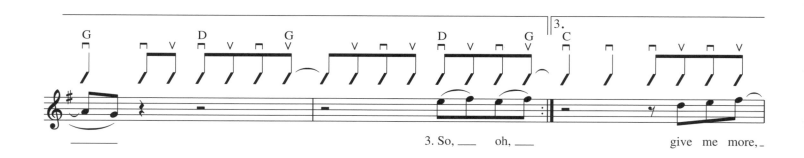

3. So, ___ oh, ___   give me more, ___

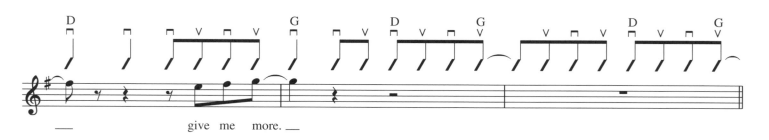

___ give me more. ___

Guitar Solo

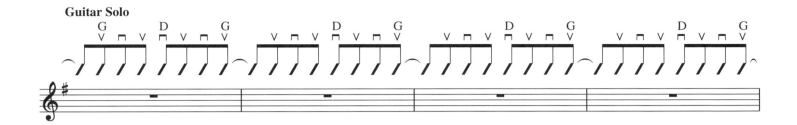

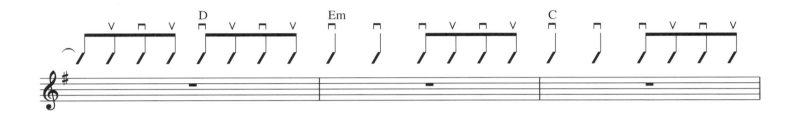

D.S. al Coda
(take 2nd ending)

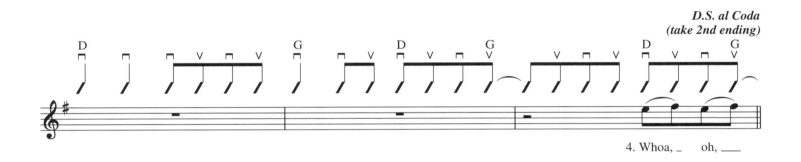

4. Whoa, __ oh, ___

⊕ Coda

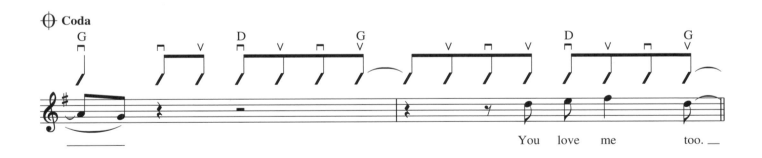

You love me too. __

Outro
Repeat and fade

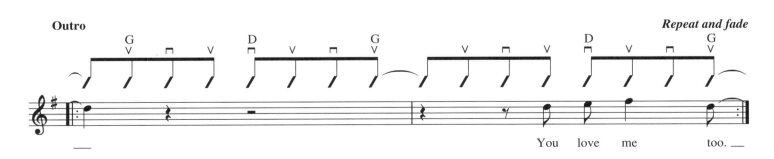

__ You love me too. __

I Saw Her Standing There

Words and Music by John Lennon and Paul McCartney

I Will

Words and Music by John Lennon and Paul McCartney

to - geth - er, love you when we're _ a - part. ___ 3. And when _

Coda

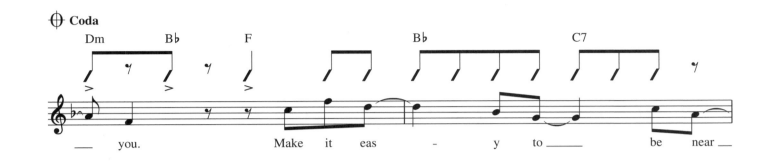

___ you. Make it eas - y to ___ be near _

___ you. For the things _ you do ___ en - dear ___ you to _ me. Ah, _

___ you know _ I will. ___ I will. _

Mm, ___ mm. _

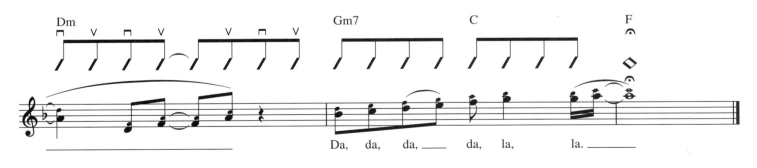

Da, da, da, ___ da, la, la. ___

I'm Only Sleeping

Words and Music by John Lennon and Paul McCartney

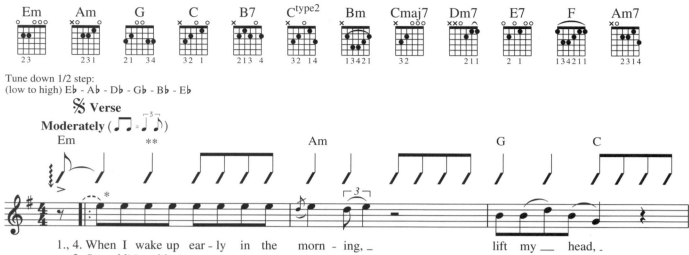

Tune down 1/2 step:
(low to high) Eb - Ab - Db - Gb - Bb - Eb

Verse

Moderately

1., 4. When I wake up ear-ly in the morn-ing, _ lift my __ head, _
2. See additional lyrics

*slur 2nd time
**3rd time, substitute E7 chord this measure.

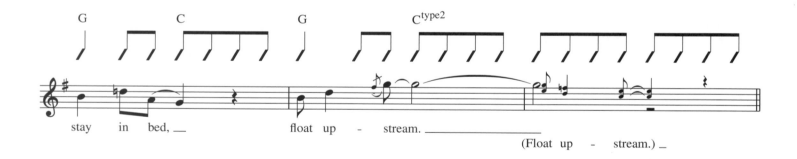

I'm still yawn-ing. ___ When I'm in the mid-dle of a dream, _

stay in bed, __ float up-stream. _____
(Float up-stream.)

Chorus

1., 3. Please don't _ wake _ me. No, ___ don't shake _ me. Leave _ me where _ I am. _
(Ooh. _____
Ooh.)

2. See additional lyrics

Please don't spoil _ my day. _ I'm miles _ a - way, _ and af - ter all, _
(Ooh. _____)

_ I'm on - ly sleep - ing. _

Bridge

Keep - ing an eye ___ on the world _

D.S. al Coda

_ go - ing by __ my __ win - dow, tak - in' my time. _ 4. When _

Coda

sleep - ing. _

Additional Lyrics

2. Ev'rybody seems to think I'm lazy.
   I don't mind, I think they're crazy.
   Runnin' ev'rywhere at such a speed,
   'Til they find there's no need. (There's no need.)

Chorus 2. Please don't spoil my day. (Ooh.)
   I'm miles away, and after all, (Ooh.)
   I'm only sleeping.

In My Life

Words and Music by John Lennon and Paul McCartney

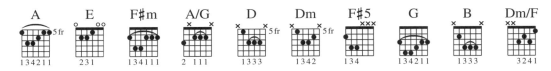

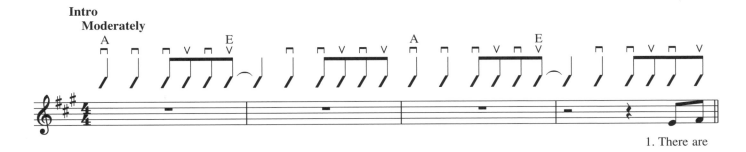

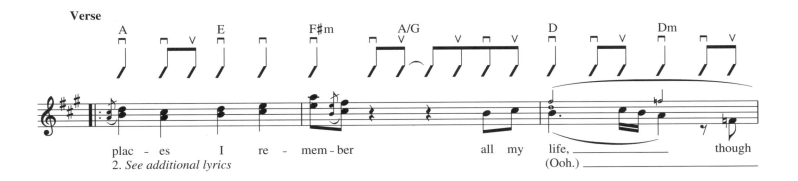

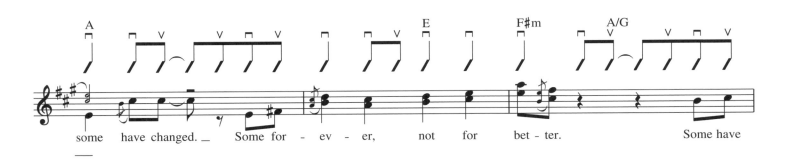

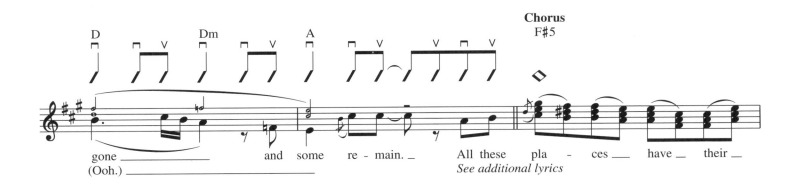

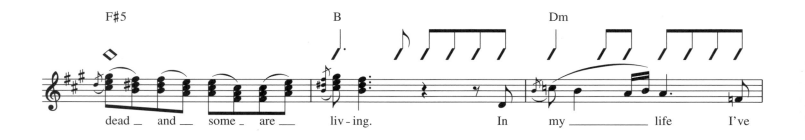

mo-ments, with lov-ers and _ friends _ I still can re - call. _ Some are

dead _ and _ some _ are _ liv - ing. In my _____ life I've

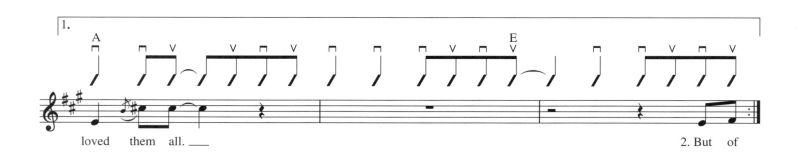

loved them all. ___ 2. But of

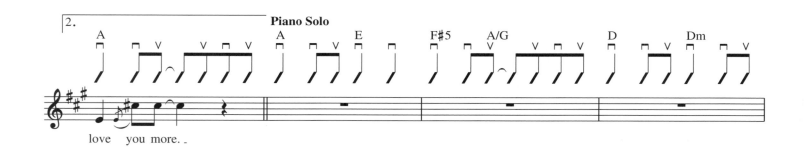

love you more. _

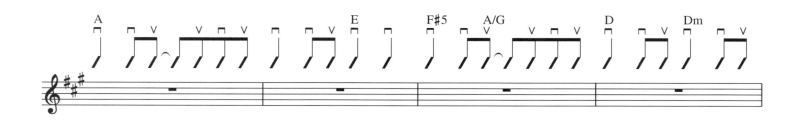

Though I know _ I'll _ nev-er lose af-fec-tion for

peo-ple and _ things _ that went be-fore, _ I know I'll of-ten stop and think a-

bout them. In my _____ life I love you more.

In my _____ life I

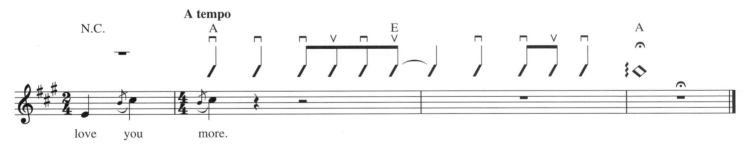

love you more.

Additional Lyrics

2. But of all these friends and lovers,
   There is no one compares with you. (Ooh.)
   And these mem'ries lose their meaning
   When I think of love as something new. (Ooh.)

Chorus Though I know I'll never lose affection
   For people and things that went before,
   I know I'll often stop and think about them.
   In my life I love you more.

Let It Be

Words and Music by John Lennon and Paul McCartney

To Coda ⊕

D.S. al Coda

⊕ **Coda**

Additional Lyrics

4. And when the night is cloudy, there is still a light that shines on me,
   Shine until tomorrow, let it be.
   I wake up to the sound of music, Mother Mary comes to me,
   Speaking words of wisdom, let it be.

Love Me Do

Words and Music by John Lennon and Paul McCartney

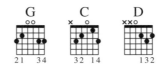

Intro
Moderately fast

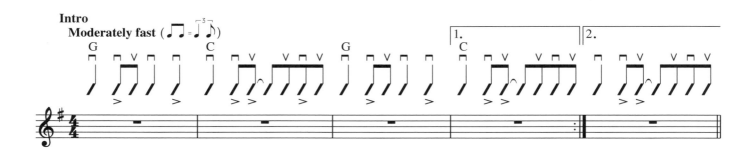

Verse

1. - 4. Love, love me do, ___ you know I love you. ___ I'll

To Coda 2

al - ways be true, ___ so ___ please ___

Chorus

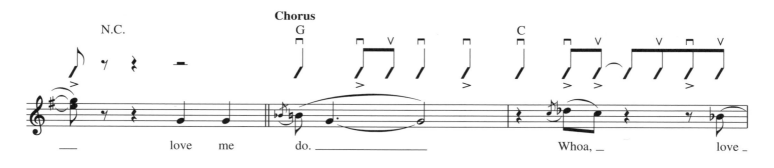

___ love me do. _____ Whoa, ___ love _

To Coda 1

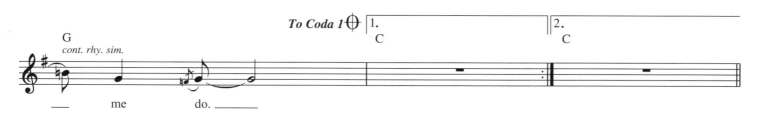

___ me do. ___

Mother Nature's Son

Words and Music by John Lennon and Paul McCartney

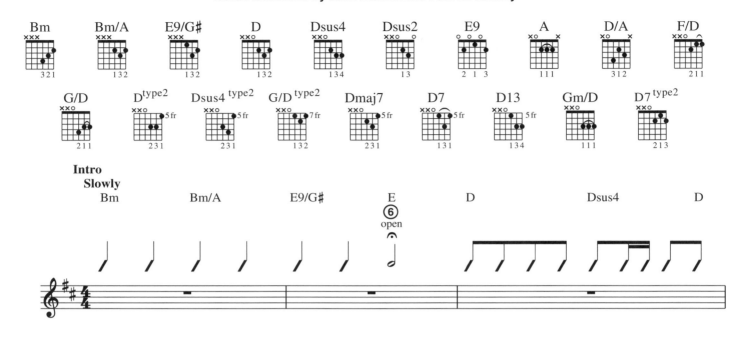

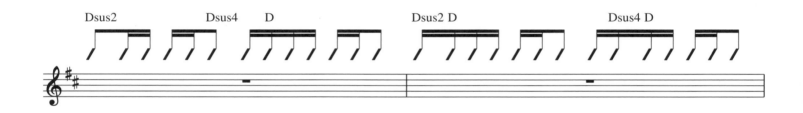

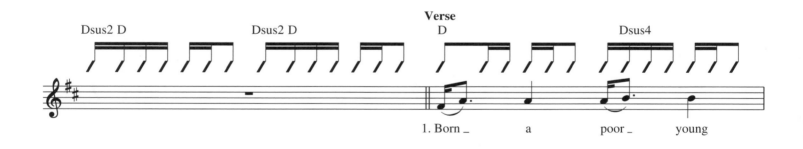

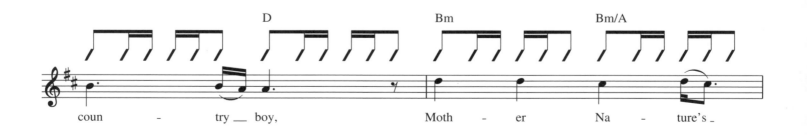

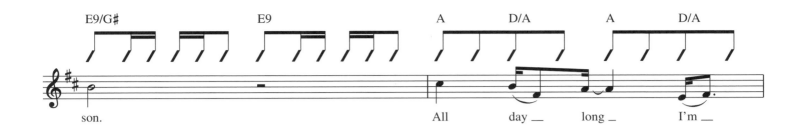

son.

All day ___ long ___ I'm ___

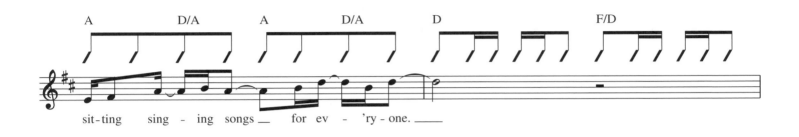

sit-ting sing - ing songs ___ for ev - 'ry - one. ___

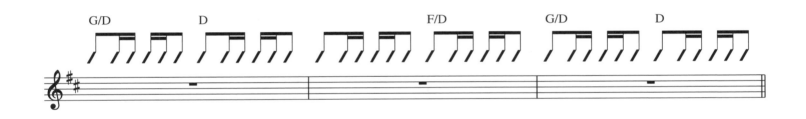

Verse

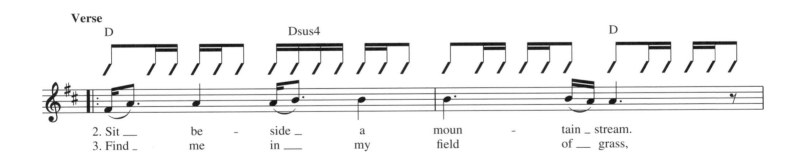

2. Sit ___ be - side ___ a moun - tain ___ stream.
3. Find ___ me in ___ my field of ___ grass,

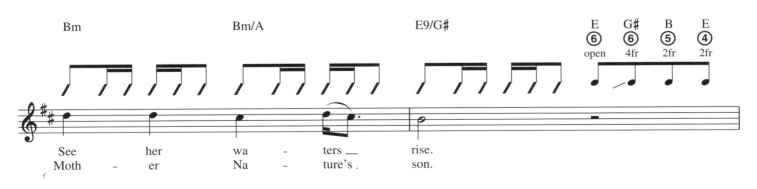

See her wa - ters ___ rise.
Moth - er Na - ture's ___ son.

37

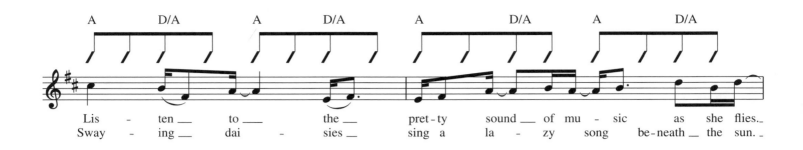

Lis - ten __ to __ the __ pret - ty sound __ of mu - sic as she flies. __
Sway - ing __ dai - sies __ sing a la - zy song be - neath __ the sun. __

Do, doot,

Bridge

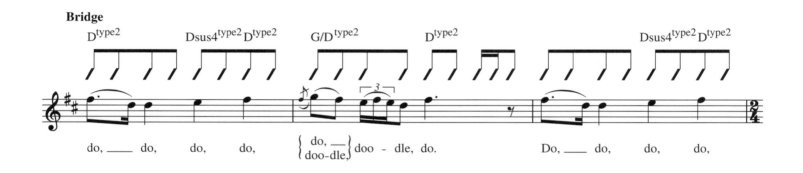

do, __ do, do, do, { do, __ / doo-dle, } doo - dle, do. Do, __ do, do, do,

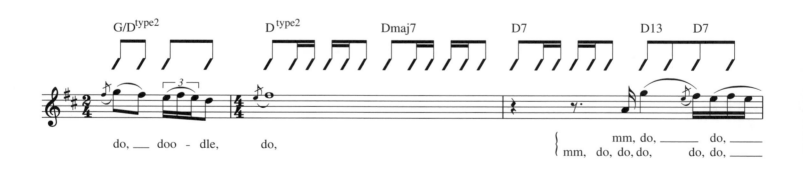

do, __ doo - dle, do, { mm, do, ___ do, ___ / mm, do, do, do, do, do, ___ }

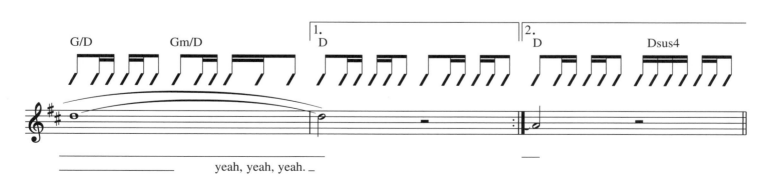

_____
_____ yeah, yeah, yeah. __

Verse

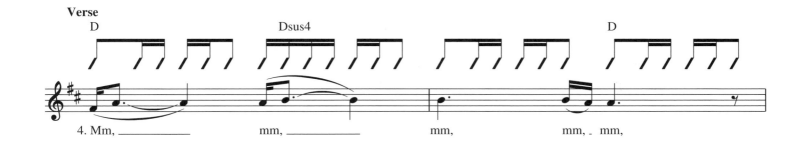

4. Mm, _____ mm, _____ mm, mm, _ mm,

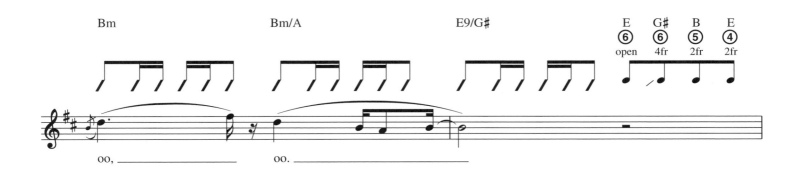

oo, _____ oo.

Mm, _____ mm, _____ mm, ____ do - wah, _

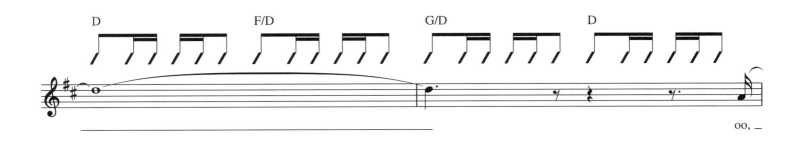

_____ oo, _

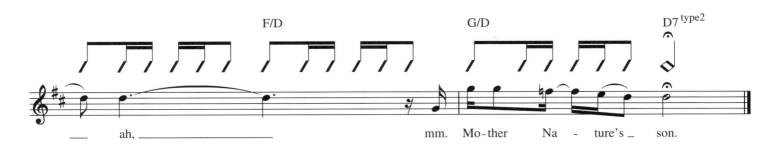

___ ah, _____ mm. Mo-ther Na - ture's _ son.

Nowhere Man

Words and Music by John Lennon and Paul McCartney

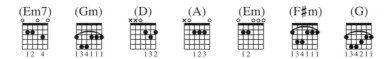

Capo II

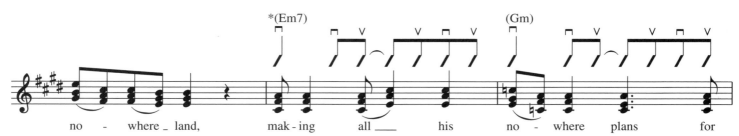

1. He's a re - al no - where _ man, sit - ting in ____ his

no - where _ land, mak - ing all ____ his no - where plans for

*Symbols in parentheses represent chord names respective to capoed guitar and do not reflect actual sounding chords.

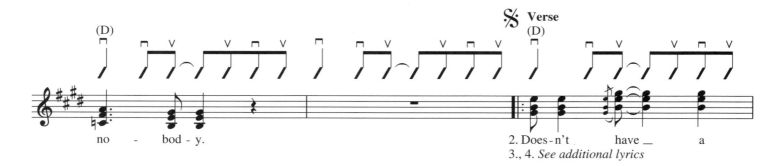

no - bod - y.

2. Does - n't have _ a

3., 4. *See additional lyrics*

point of view, _ knows not where he's go - ing to. ____

*Symbols in parentheses represent chord names respective to capoed guitar.
Symbols above reflect actual sounding chords.

Is - n't he ____ a bit ____ like you ____ and me? _____

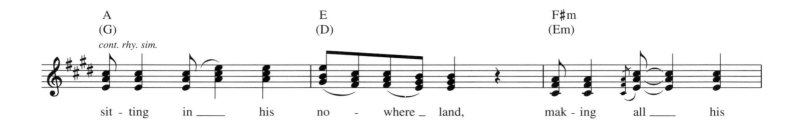

sit - ting in ____ his no - where ____ land, mak - ing all ____ his

no - where plans for no - bod - y. Mak - ing all ____ his

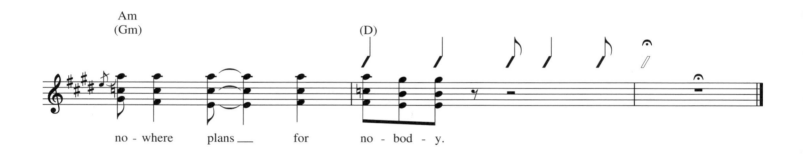

no - where plans ____ for no - bod - y.

Additional Lyrics

3. He's as blind as he can be,
   Just sees what he wants to see.
   Nowhere man can you see me at all?

Bridge Nowhere man don't worry. (Ah, la, la, la.)
   Take your time don't hurry. (Ah, la, la, la.)
   Leave it all (Ah, la, la, la.)
   'Til somebody else lends you a hand. (Ah, la, la, la, la.)

4. Doesn't have a point of view,
   Knows not where he's going to.
   Isn't he a bit like you and me?

Rocky Raccoon

Words and Music by John Lennon and Paul McCartney

shoot off the legs of his riv - al. His r' riv-al, it seems, had
"Dan-na boy, this is a show - down." But Dan-iel was hot. Ah, he

brok-en his dreams by steal-ing the girl of his fan - cy. Her
drew first and shot and

name was Ma-gil and she called her-self Lil, but ev-'ry-one knew her as Nan-

cy. 3. Now, Rock-y col-lapsed in the cor - ner.

Piano Solo

Da, 'n' da, da, da, da, da, da, da. Da, 'n' da, da, da, da, da, da, da. da,

'n' la, da, da, da, da, da, da, da, da, da, da, da, da, da, da, do, 'n' do, do, do, doo -

- dle, do, do, do, do, do, do, do, doo - dle, do, do, do, do, do, do, do, do,

doo-dle-oo, do doo-dle, do, do, doo-dle do, 'n' doo-dle-eh la, da, 'n' doo-dle, do, do, doot. 4. Now, the

Verse

doc - tor came in stink - ing of gin and pro -

ceed - ed to lie on the ta - ble. He said,

44

Sgt. Pepper's Lonely Hearts Club Band

Words and Music by John Lennon and Paul McCartney

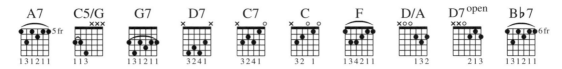

Intro
Moderate Rock

(Audience and orchestra warmup ambience)

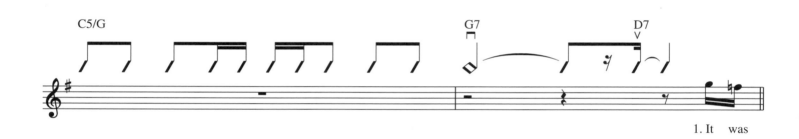

1. It was

Verse

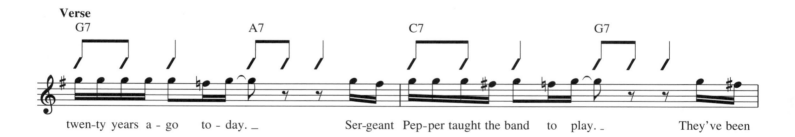

twen-ty years a - go to - day. __ Ser-geant Pep-per taught the band to play. __ They've been

go-ing in and out of style, __ but they're guar-an-teed to raise a smile. __ So

may I in-tro-duce to you __ the act you've known for all these years? _____

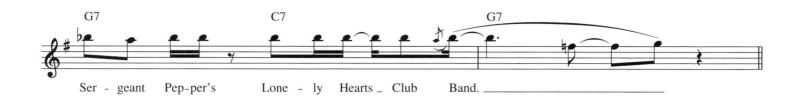

Ser - geant Pep-per's Lone - ly Hearts _ Club Band. _____

Interlude

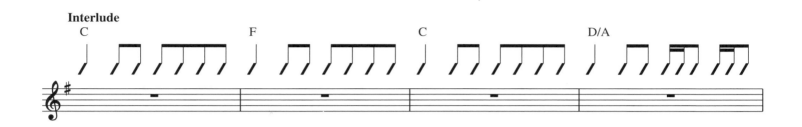

Chorus

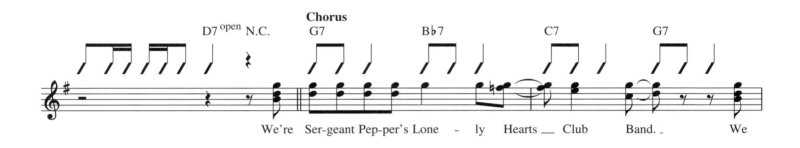

We're Ser-geant Pep-per's Lone - ly Hearts _ Club Band. _ We

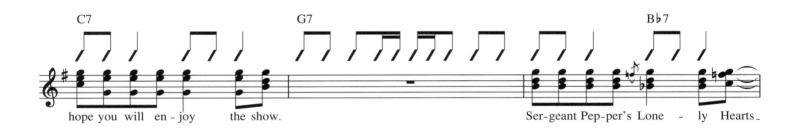

hope you will en - joy the show. Ser-geant Pep-per's Lone - ly Hearts _

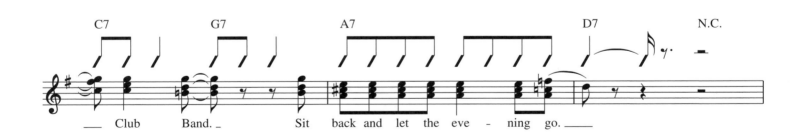

_ Club Band. _ Sit back and let the eve - ning go. _____

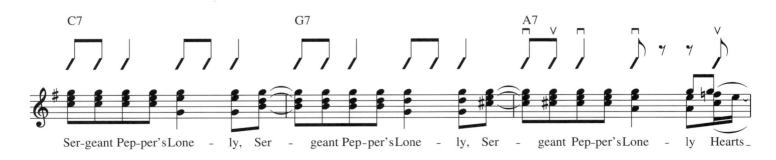

Ser-geant Pep-per's Lone - ly, Ser - geant Pep-per's Lone - ly, Ser - geant Pep-per's Lone - ly Hearts _

Bridge

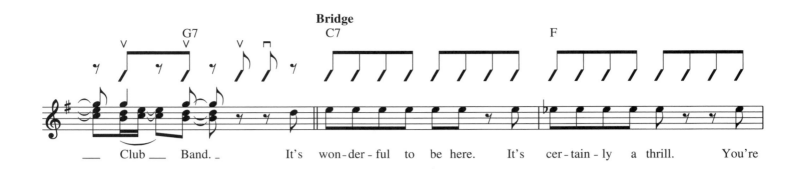

__ Club __ Band. _   It's won-der-ful to be here.   It's cer-tain-ly a thrill.   You're

such a love-ly au-di-ence, we'd like to take you home with us. We'd love to take you home.   2. I don't

Verse

real-ly want to stop the show.   But I thought you might like to know _   that the

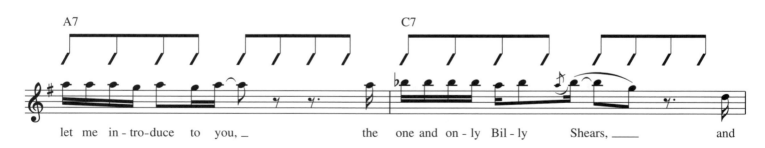

sing-er's gon-na sing a song _   and he wants you all to sing a - long. _   So

let me in-tro-duce to you, _   the one and on-ly Bil-ly Shears, _____ and

Segue to "With a Little Help From My Friends"

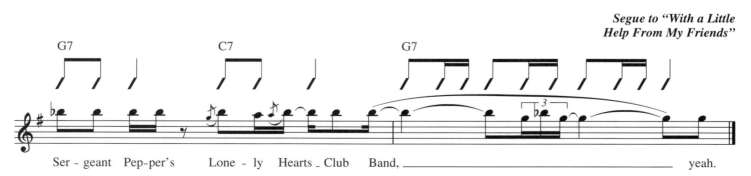

Ser - geant Pep-per's   Lone - ly Hearts _ Club Band, _____ yeah.

She Loves You

Words and Music by John Lennon and Paul McCartney

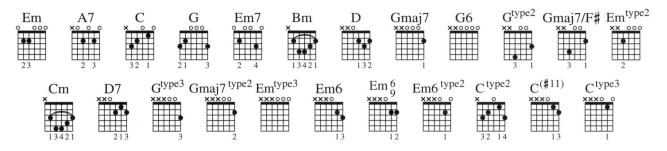

Intro-Chorus
Moderately fast

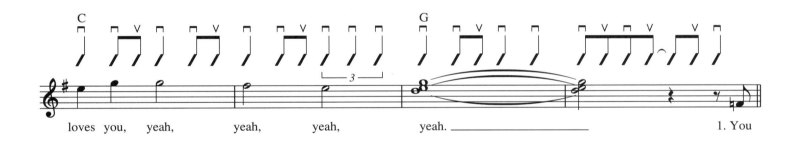

She loves you, yeah, yeah, yeah. She loves you, yeah, yeah, yeah. She

loves you, yeah, yeah, yeah, yeah. 1. You

Verse

think you've lost your love, ____ well, I saw her yes-ter-day. ____ It's
said you hurt her so, ____ she al-most lost her mind. ____ But
know it's up to you, ____ I think it's on-ly fair. ____

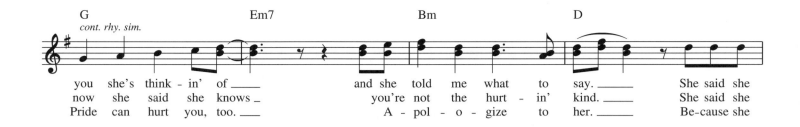

you she's think-in' of _____ and she told me what to say. _____ She said she
now she said she knows _ you're not the hurt-in' kind. _____ She said she
Pride can hurt you, too. _____ A-pol-o-gize to her. _____ Be-cause she

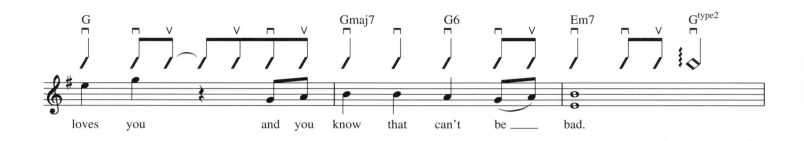

loves you and you know that can't be _____ bad.

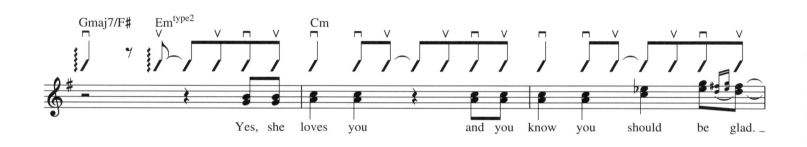

Yes, she loves you and you know you should be glad. _

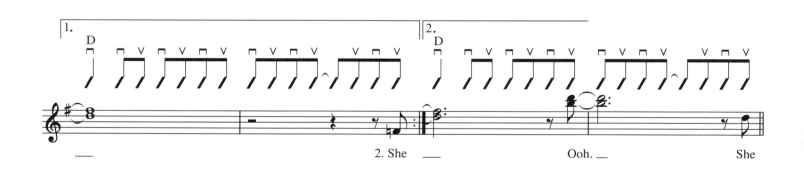

_____ 2. She _____ Ooh. _ She

Chorus

loves you, yeah, yeah, yeah. _ She loves you, yeah, yeah, yeah. _ With a

To Coda ⊕

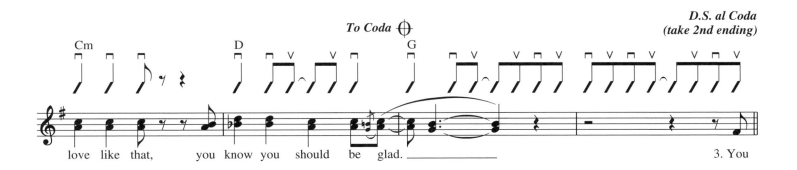

love like that,   you know you should   be glad. _____   3. You

⊕ **Coda**

With a   love   like   that,   you know you should   be glad. __

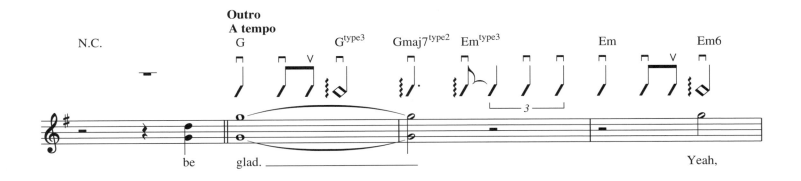

With a   love   like   that,   you know   you should _____

Outro
A tempo

be   glad. _____   Yeah,

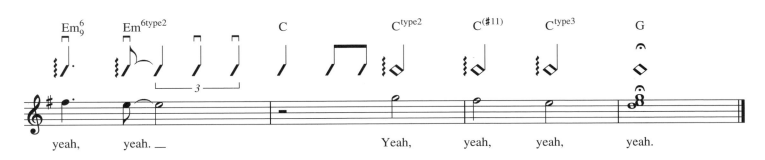

yeah,   yeah. __   Yeah,   yeah,   yeah,   yeah.

Something

Words and Music by George Harrison

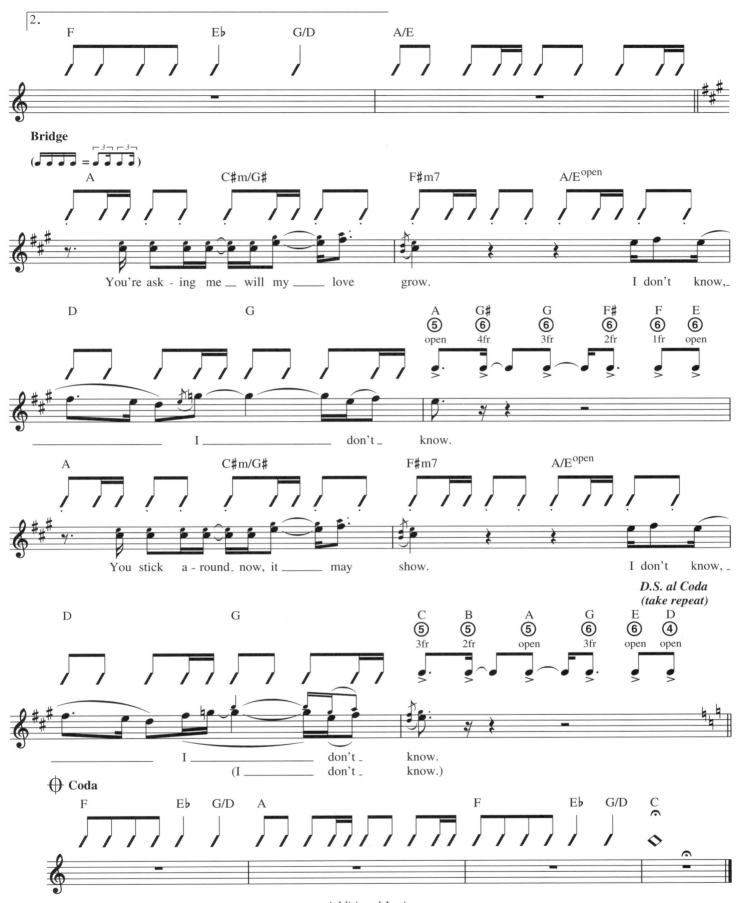

Additional Lyrics

2. Somewhere in her smile she knows
That I don't need no other lover.
Something in the style that shows me.
I don't want to leave her now,
You know I believe and how.

4. Something in the way she knows,
And all I have to do is think of her.
Something in the things she shows me.
I don't want to leave her now,
You know I believe and how.

We Can Work It Out

Words and Music by John Lennon and Paul McCartney

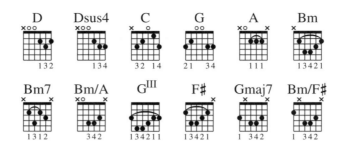

Verse
Moderately slow

1. Try to see it my way. Do I have to keep on talk-ing
2. Think of what your say - ing. You can get it wrong and still you think

'til I can't go on? While you see it your way,
that it's al - right. Think of what I'm say - ing.

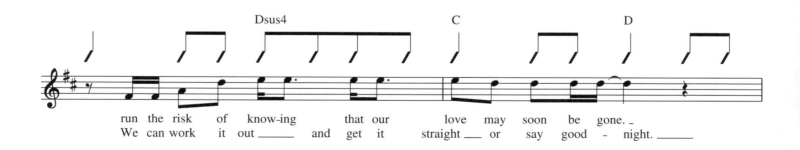

run the risk of know-ing that our love may soon be gone.
We can work it out and get it straight or say good - night.

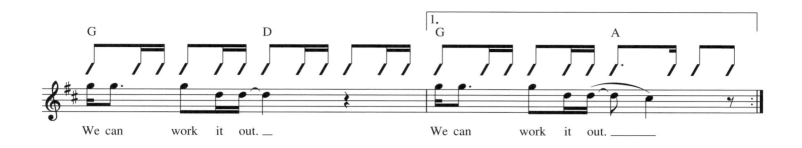

We can work it out. ___ We can work it out. _____

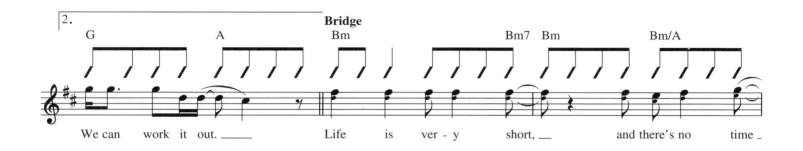

We can work it out. _____ Life is ver-y short, __ and there's no time _

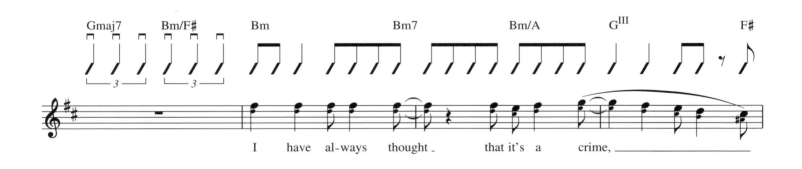

_____ for fuss-ing and fight-ing, my friend.

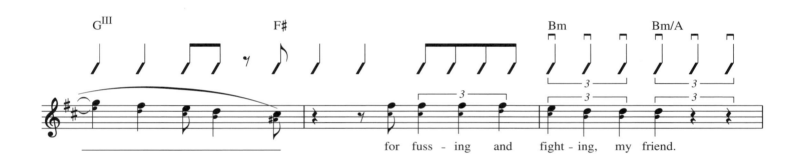

I have al-ways thought _ that it's a crime, _____

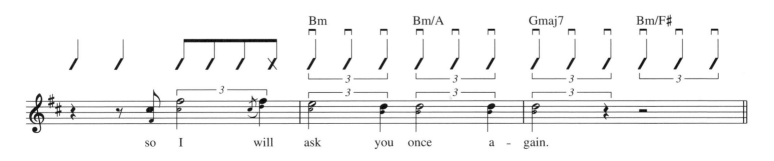

so I will ask you once a-gain.

Verse

D Dsus4 D Dsus4

3., 4. Try to see it my way. _ On - ly time will tell __ if I __ am

C D Dsus4 D

right or I am wrong. While you see it your way, _

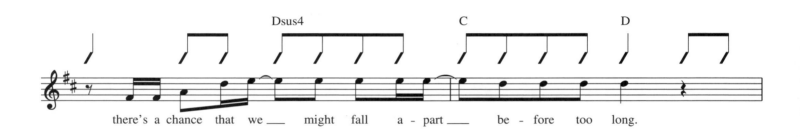

Dsus4 C D

there's a chance that we __ might fall a - part __ be - fore too long.

To Coda ⊕

G D G A

We can work it out. _ We can work it out. ____

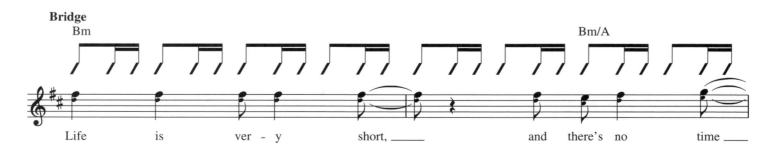

Bridge

Bm Bm/A

Life is ver - y short, ____ and there's no time ____

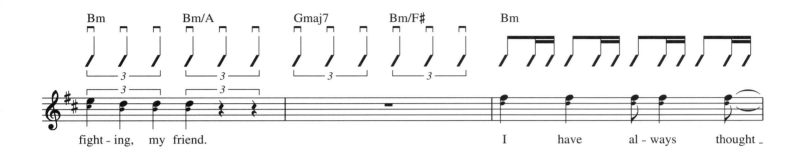

for fuss - ing and

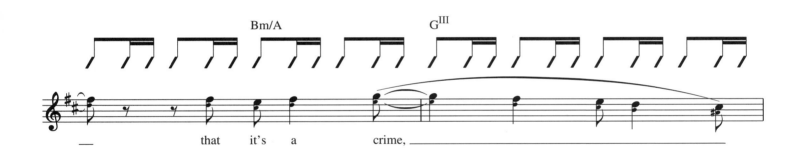

fight - ing, my friend.   I   have   al - ways   thought

that   it's   a   crime,

D.S. al Coda

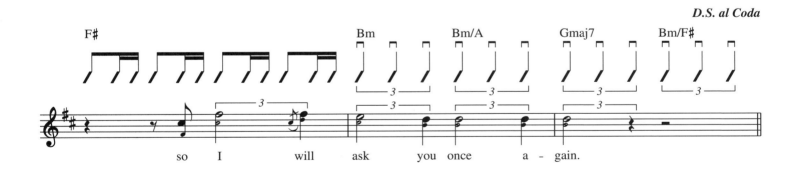

so   I   will   ask   you   once   a - gain.

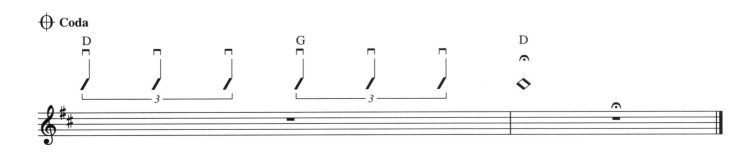

Yesterday

Words and Music by John Lennon and Paul McCartney

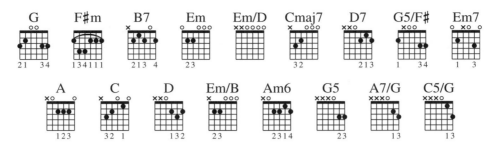

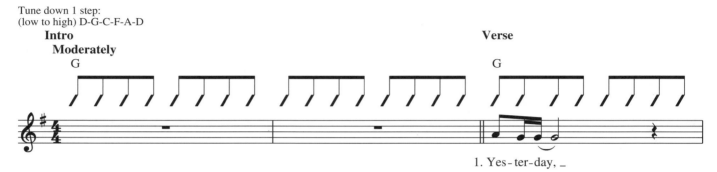

Tune down 1 step:
(low to high) D-G-C-F-A-D

Intro
Moderately

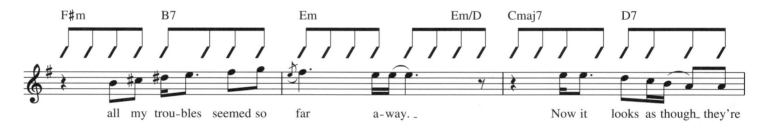

1. Yes-ter-day, _

all my trou-bles seemed so far a-way. _ Now it looks as though_ they're

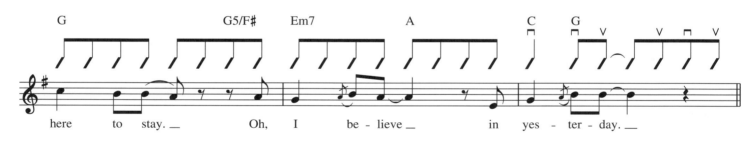

here to stay. _ Oh, I be-lieve _ in yes-ter-day. _

Verse

cont. rhy. sim.

2. Sud-den-ly, _____ I'm not half the man _ I used to be.
3. Yes-ter-day, _____ love was such an eas-y game to play. _

There's a shad-ow hang-ing o-ver me. __ Oh, __ yes-ter-day __ came
Now I need_ a place to hide a-way. __ Oh, __ I be-lieve _ in

You've Got to Hide Your Love Away

Words and Music by John Lennon and Paul McCartney

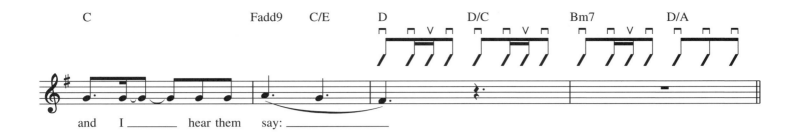

C   Fadd9   C/E   D   D/C   Bm7   D/A

and   I _____ hear them   say: _____

Chorus

G   C   Dsus4   D   Dsus2

Hey! ___   You've got to hide   your ___ love a - way. _____

D   G   C

cont. rhy. sim.

Hey! ___   You've got to   hide   your ___ love a -

2nd time, D.S. al Coda

Dsus4   D   Dsus2   D

⊕ **Coda**

Fadd9   C   G

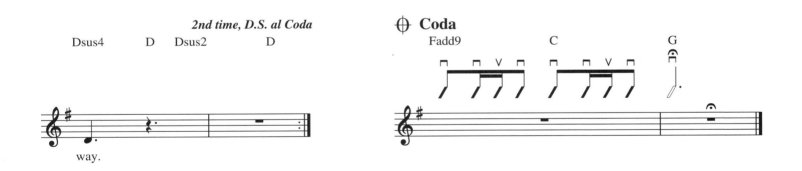

way.

Additional Lyrics

2. How can I even try, I can never win.
    Hearing them, seeing them, in the state I'm in.
    How could she say to me love will find a way?
    Gather 'round all you clowns, let me hear you say:

While My Guitar Gently Weeps

Words and Music by George Harrison

*Sing 1st time only.